THE SOUTHERN REGION IN THE 1970S AND 1980S

Andy Gibbs

AMBERLEY

Front cover above: Clattering through the Hampshire countryside, No. 33026 is photographed at Lee with 1O41, the 12.10 Cardiff Central to Portsmouth Harbour service, on 2 May 1988. (P. Barber)

Front cover below: 1O74, the 07.44 Manchester Piccadilly to Brighton, approaches Patcham Tunnel on the outskirts of Brighton in the summer of 1980. Crewe-allocated No. 47492 has charge of the train on this day. (A. Gibbs)

Back Cover: 4CIG No. 1294 leads a twelve-car formation at Copyhold Junction, just north of Haywards Heath, on 1 August 1987. The train is working the 10.05 Victoria to Brighton fast service. The line leading off to the right is the former branch to Horsted Keynes, which is still in use and goes as far as an aggregates terminal at Ardingly station. (M. Hull)

First published 2018

Amberley Publishing
The Hill, Stroud
Gloucestershire, GL5 4EP

www.amberley-books.com

Copyright © Andy Gibbs, 2018

The right of Andy Gibbs to be identified as the Author of this work has been asserted in accordance with the Copyrights, Designs and Patents Act 1988.

ISBN 978 1 4456 8143 6 (print)
ISBN 978 1 4456 8144 3 (ebook)

British Library Cataloguing in Publication Data.
A catalogue record for this book is available from the British Library.

Origination by Amberley Publishing.
Printed in the UK.

Introduction

While I was born just before the *Evening Star* was built, steam engines never had a great fascination for me. Nevertheless, I grew up with a love of anything on wheels, especially trains – not helped by my Dad, who had worked for the SR and later Brighton, Hove & District/Southdown. Living in Brighton meant there was a decent train service in all directions (except south). During the 1970s, once I acquired a camera, school holidays meant cheap Runabout tickets to get to more exotic locations like Southampton or Ashford! Later on the Young Persons Railcard, and later still the British Rail free passes and privilege tickets, meant that my travels expanded further still.

The Southern Region of British Rail was not all third rail EMUs, although it often seems like it. There was a huge variety of freight and inter-regional workings that brought 'foreign' locomotives in to the area and these were much more of a lure to me.

This volume has pictures that at the time seemed mundane and ordinary; the BR Blue era has long gone and unfortunately so has the variety of trains.

Some of the photographs are taken by me but most come from my library. The price of transparency film at the time limited what photographs I could take; a 36-exposure film had to last a week, and then, if you were lucky, you had another week's wait for the results to come back from the developers.

This will be the first in a series of regional books, but my old stomping ground of Brighton and Sussex will be covered more fully in a separate volume as I've probably enough images for five or six. I hope the pictures will take you back to those times to enjoy British Rail as it was through the 1970s and '80s in all its grubbiness.

I would like to thank everyone I've worked with on British Rail and later in the privatised rail industry; you know who you are and it's been a pleasure. I'd also like to thank my wife, who has had to put up with this obsession over the years, even though she was a BR employee herself.

A clean-looking No. 33051 passes through the Up centre road at Ashford (Kent) with a mixed bag of international wagons from the train ferry at Dover, bound for the London Midland Region via Maidstone East, in September 1981.

Ashford was the limit of an SR Runabout ticket, which allowed me to get from Brighton across the marsh during the school holidays. In 1974, No. 08156 trundles through Ashford (Kent) with a permanent way crane and match wagon, and a couple of 16-ton mineral wagons bringing up the rear. (A. Gibbs)

Passing at speed through the centre road at Ashford (Kent) in 1978 is 4CEP unit No. 7174, leading a twelve-car formation on a Victoria to Dover Western Docks service. Passengers on this train were bound for the connection via the Sealink ferry to Calais.

On a grey autumn day, we find 4CEP unit No. 7176 approaching Ashford (Kent) while working a Ramsgate to Charing Cross service via Canterbury West service. 8 October 1981.

The Southern Region was very quick to reform units as circumstances dictated. Here we find 3R 'Tadpole' unit No. 1206 waiting to depart Ashford with a train to Hastings. The 3R units were formed in 1964 by disbanding 6S units Nos 1002 to 1004, using the power cars and trailer seconds plus a driving trailer from a 2EPB unit. 9 October 1981.

No. 47246 takes a train of empty Tarmac PGA aggregate hoppers through Ashford (Kent) on a bright autumn day. 9 October 1981.

The Hastings to Ashford line has always held a fascination due to its DEMU services; here we find 3H unit No. 1114 arriving at Ashford (Kent) on 9 October 1981.

Arriving in the mist at Rye on 24 March 1987 is 4L DEMU No. 203001 with the 12.44 departure from Ashford (Kent) to Hastings. This unit had been reduced to a four-car train in May 1986 and was renumbered from 1011 in January of 1987.

To the east of Ashford station was a small stabling point, in which could often be found a collection of locomotives from Classes 33, 71 and 73. In 1974, we find No. 71003 running into the sidings. (A. Gibbs)

On a misty day in March, 3H unit No. 205101 passes 4L No. 203001 at Rye station while working the 12.45 from Hastings to Ashford (Kent) on 24 March 1987.

3H DEMU No. 205024 departs from the deserted and uninviting station at Winchelsea with a service from Hastings to Ashford (Kent) on 28 November 1988. Like many villages, the station is remote from the location it is named after.

At Ore station on 9 October 1981 we find 2HAP No. 6053 arriving with a sister unit to form a service to Brighton. The train has just been shunted across from the adjacent platform. Access sidings to the carriage shed can be seen to the left of the train.

Filling the station with exhaust on 27 August 1977, 6L unit No. 1031 can be seen at Hastings. In the background an unidentified 4CIG has arrived from Victoria, there is an unidentified 3H DEMU and either another 3H or a 2HAP. The goods yard is still in use; a few wagons litter the sidings along with various permanent way road vans and Rail Express Parcels delivery vans.

It's not the nicest of days in Hastings as 3H DEMU No. 1111 waits to depart with a service to Ashford (Kent) on 6 October 1981.

A grey morning in Tonbridge in 1977 sees No. 33208 rattle through the station with a long train of ferry vans and wagons from the train ferry at Dover. The headcode BA denotes a service bound for the London Midland Region via Tonbridge.

In Tonbridge West yard on 24 May 1980 we find Class 73 electro-diesel No. 73122, with a couple of unidentified shunters in the background.

The secondman looks back from 'Slim Jim' Class 33 No. 33211 as it trundles through Gravesend station with a permanent way train in 1977. The first wagon's sides are literally bulging at the seams with ballast spoil.

Approaching Crayford station we find No. 73128 in charge of a train of bogie aggregate hoppers on 25 May 1981.

The 4EPB units were the suburban workhorses for most of South and South East London; here we find unit No. 5487 at Grove Park station in July 1978.

Hither Green Depot in Lewisham was home to approximately half the Class 33 fleet, including all the Hastings line gauge Class 33/2s. Here we find No. 33212 and a couple of sister locos basking in the sunshine in May 1981.

A pair of unidentified 'Slim Jim' Class 33/2s rest at Hither Green Depot between duties in May 1981.

The scene around London Bridge and the station itself have changed immensely in the last few years. Here on Platform 4, 2HAP unit No. 6068 forms part of a Charing Cross to Dartford via Bexleyheath service on 7 October 1981.

Refurbished 4CEP unit No. 411603 is captured in the bright sunshine at London Bridge while working a Charing Cross to Margate service on 7 October 1981.

Smart-looking Hastings DEMU No. 1011 is at London Bridge with a Charing Cross to Hastings service on 7 October 1981.

SR-designed 4EPB No. 5005 pauses at London Bridge with a Charing Cross to Gillingham service on 7 October 1981.

A gala weekend was held to commemorate the 150th anniversary of the London & Greenwich Railway. Here at Cannon Street station, and among the exhibits, South Western Division unit No. 455872, newly repainted into NSE livery, departs with a special shuttle service to Charing Cross on 23 August 1986. King Arthur Class *Sir Lamiel* and No. 56047 can be glimpsed in the background.

London has an ever changing skyline and here we can see a view that has changed hugely since this image was taken from St Paul's in 1982. Blackfriars Bridge now sports a new station as part of the Thameslink project. The right-hand bridge was removed and Ludgate House, the new offices for the *Daily Express* built on the approach, is now in the process of being demolished. A pair of 4EPB units can be seen berthed in the sidings. 24 April 1982.

Approaching Blackfriars station from the long-gone Holborn Viaduct station is SR 4EPB unit No. 5188 on a working to Swanley on 10 March 1983. In the sidings is BR 2EPB unit No. 5747.

Standing under the train shed at Charing Cross as part of a train working to Caterham and Tattenham Corner on 26 August 1978 is SR 2EPB unit No. 5651. Charing Cross now has a large office block above the platforms and this service was cut back to start from London Bridge a few years ago.

There obviously hasn't been much litter picking on the platforms at Victoria recently, as displayed by the rubbish-covered tracks that surround SR 4EPB units Nos 5107 and 5485, both of which are seen sporting NSE flashes. A large crowd of people to the right wait to board a boat train on Platform 1. 24 August 1986. (M. Hull)

The VSOE British Pullman has become a bit of a railway institution since its inauguration in 1982. Here we see Class 73 No. 73130, having just arrived and being attached to the train, ready to depart from Victoria for the run down to Folkestone Harbour on 18 August 1986. (I. J. Stewart)

While the central division side of Victoria has long been dark and gloomy, the eastern side remains without any overhead development. On September 1982 we see an unidentified Class 73 departing with the Venice Simplon-Orient-Express to exotic Folkestone, with onward connections to Calais, Paris, Milan and, of course, Venice.

Stewarts Lane Depot is hemmed in by the maze of railway lines in the Battersea area of South London and has been home to many of the Southern Region's diesel and electric locomotives. No. 33006 is captured by itself in the sunshine on 16 September 1977. (P. Barber)

From the May 1986 timetable a new group of cross-country trains were introduced from the North West via Kensington Olympia to Kent and improved services to Sussex. At Canterbury East we find 1M22, the 13.55 Dover Western Docks to Liverpool Lime Street, about to depart with large logo-liveried No. 47518 in charge in November 1987.

On a grey 6 October 1981 at Ramsgate station we find 4CEP unit No. 7201 departing.

The 4CEP units were the mainstay of the Kent Coast electrification from 1957 until their replacement by Class 375s early this century. At its home depot station of Ramsgate, unit No. 7191 is seen arriving on a service from Margate to Charing Cross on 6 October 1981.

It's 2 p.m. on 6 March 1982 and a couple of passengers hurry along the platform at Dover Western Docks station. In the platform we see 4VEP No. 7763 and 4CEP No. 7205. (R. Marsh)

Looking along the western arm of Dover Harbour in 1975 we can see a 2HAP and a 4CEP in the carriage shed. Out in open are a pair of Class 33s, one of which is coupled to the Victoria Travelling Post Office stock, formed of former Southern Railway vehicles.

At Shakespeare Cliff, with the English Channel alongside, we find solitary 4CEP unit No. 1531 en route to Charing Cross in August 1982.

Class 33 No. 33205 is seen coupled to the coaches of the Dover to Stirling Motorail service on 6 June 1981. This train conveyed passengers in sleepers or first-class seats, with their cars loaded onto flat wagons. This train was combined with a similar portion from Brockenhurst at Kensington Olympia for the overnight journey to Scotland.

The direct trains from the North West and Midlands into Kent didn't take off as expected and were subject to numerous route and destination changes prior to withdrawal. In the second year of service, No. 47611 *Thames* in InterCity livery has charge of 1M31, the 17.54 from Dover Western Docks to Manchester Piccadilly, in April 1988.

Before the central side platforms of Victoria station disappeared under the shopping centre, No. 73128 and a Gatwick Express set are seen illuminated by the light managing to get through the glass of the train shed on 24 August 1986. (M. Hull)

During the ASLEF strikes of July 1982 there were some weird and wonderful services using the few drivers that were still working. One involved a six-car DMU formed of Class 119 Gloucester Cross-Country sets between Brighton and Victoria. Here we see set L572 on the stops of Platform 10 at Victoria sometime between 5 July and 18 July 1982. (A. Edwards)

May 1984 saw the start of the dedicated Gatwick Express service running non-stop between Victoria and Gatwick Airport. A month into the service we find No. 73129 *City of Winchester* having just arrived at Victoria. The shopping centre raft above the station has yet to be built. (P. Barber)

Fast forward to 11 April 1987 and the central side of Victoria is now buried under the shopping centre. No. 73107 and a short winter five-car Gatwick Express formation lurk in the gloom.

Taken from Latchmere Junction signal box in 1981, No. 47225 rounds the curve from Clapham Junction and starts to accelerate away with 1M64, the 15.00 Brighton to Manchester Piccadilly.

Another image taken from Latchmere Junction signal box; in glorious sunshine, an unidentified Class 47/4 coasts through the junction with 1M64, the 15.00 Brighton to Manchester Piccadilly, on March 1982.

Clapham Junction, as the busiest station in the country, has always been a Mecca for trainspotters, the huge variety of services through the station being the main attraction. Here we find 3D DEMU No. 207012 leading a sister unit through the station on a Victoria to East Grinstead service on 1 October 1987.

The 1986 timetable saw a big boost to the inter-city service between Brighton and the Midlands, with all services now booked to call at Clapham Junction. The driver of No. 47609 *Firefly* looks back for the 'RA' while working 1M00, the 13.22 Brighton to Liverpool Lime Street, on 1 October 1987. Next stop, Kensington Olympia.

4EPB No. 5424 rounds the curve into Clapham Junction while working a Victoria to Epsom Downs service on1 October 1987.

No. 73122 *County of East Sussex* powers through Clapham Junction with a Victoria to Gatwick service on 1 October 1987.

No. 47622 *The Institute of Mechanical Engineers* gets away from Clapham Junction with 1O74, the 11.55 Manchester Piccadilly to Brighton inter-city service, on 7 May 1988. The serpentine nature of Platform 16 at Clapham Junction has always made train despatch difficult with a long train.

An unidentified Class 47/4 passes through Balham station with 1M64, the 15.07 from Brighton to Manchester Piccadilly, in September 1980. A suburban train formed of EPB stock departs southwards.

Class 33 No. 6555 (later No. 33037) is captured passing through Tooting Bec Common at Balham with a long freight train from Norwood Junction bound for the Eastern Region in April 1975. (S. Creer)

Inside part of Selhurst Depot in 1972 we find, from left to right, an unidentified 4SUB, 2EPB unit No. 5665, 4SUB unit No. 4732 and 2EPB unit No. 5607. 4SUB No. 4732 remained in service long after the rest of the class were withdrawn and scrapped and remains preserved but in poor condition.

Depot open days were a common thing during the 1970s and '80s, and that even included the Southern with the dangers of the third rail. This is the 1980 Selhurst open day and Class 50 No. 50023 *Howe* and No. 47581 *Great Eastern* are among the exhibits on 21 September 1980. (A. Gibbs)

Selhurst Depot was host to several open days during the 1970s and '80s. Here at the September 1980 open day we find a Class 33, a Class 119 DMU and 4EPB No. 5143. (A. Gibbs)

An unidentified Class 73 is used to demonstrate an overhead crane at Selhurst Depot during the September 1980 open day. Note that there are no barriers around the locomotive. (A. Gibbs)

Selhurst Depot open day 1978 and at the depot entrance we see No. 73133, possibly Stratford's No. 47164 and other exhibits, including an instruction saloon, various air-braked wagons, a Class 33 and another Class 73. (A. Edwards)

During the 1980s there were very few loco-hauled services on the Central division and these were mainly restricted to the Oxted line serving East Grinstead and Uckfield in the peaks. At London Bridge in 1982 we find Crompton No. 33064 waiting to depart with 2U14, the 17.20 to Uckfield.

Climbing up from West Norwood to Tulse Hill in the winter of 1980 we find Crewe-allocated No. 47483 with 1M50, the 09.20 Brighton to Manchester Piccadilly. The train was diverted this way due to engineering work. After East Croydon the next stop was Reading. Journey time from Brighton was only an hour and forty-five minutes. (A. Gibbs)

Looking north from New Cross Gate station on 30 October 1980, we find No. 08655 in charge of a few engineer's wagons. The extensive sidings and yards here were removed to be replaced by a supermarket and later by the London Overground Depot.

No. 33064 heads north through New Cross Gate station with a single Mk 1 BSK in tow on 30 October 1980. To the left is an unidentified 3H DEMU, and to the right are various stabled 4CIG EMUs.

Approaching Norwood Junction station in bright autumn sun on 30 October 1980 is SR 2SAP unit No. 5614 on a London Bridge to Epsom Downs service.

In a cloud of exhaust, Class 25 No. 25301 rattles into Norwood Junction station with an inter-regional freight, probably from Willesden, in 1980. The train has a single Presflo cement wagon behind the loco, followed by an open wagon and a few Class A tank wagons.

Departing Norwood Junction in 1980 is 4EPB unit No. 5225 with an unidentified London-bound service.

No. 33008 has charge of an engineer's train at Norwood Junction on 6 August 1976. The headcode 7G suggests it's bound for Coulsdon North.

The platform staff at Norwood Junction give the guard the 'right away'. 4EPB unit No. 5017 and an unidentified 2EPB unit are en route from Charing Cross to Caterham and Tattenham Corner when seen in 1980.

An unidentified Class 33/0 accelerates through East Croydon station with a train of tank wagons in September 1979. The headcode of FO hopefully means it's a train heading from the Eastern Region towards Brighton! (A. Edwards)

The track layout at East Croydon was very different prior to the Brighton line resignalling scheme. Here we find 4VEG unit No. 7904 about to leave Platform 4 on a Littlehampton to Victoria service via Horsham on 14 March 1981. In Platform 3 No. 47440 waits to depart with 1M50, the 09.20 Brighton to Manchester Piccadilly.

Crewe-allocated No. 47440 waits to depart from East Croydon with 1M50, the 09.20 Brighton to Manchester Piccadilly, on 14 March 1981. In just under an hour the train would be at Reading, its next port of call.

A snowy winter's day and a smartly turned out but unidentified Class 47/0 passes through East Croydon station on February 1979 with a train of tank wagons, which are probably bound for Salfords or Selsdon. (A. Edwards)

Unusual power for a Victoria to Brighton service, but it is an ASLEF strike day. Class 119 DMU set No. 571 has been borrowed from its usual Gatwick to Reading run for the day and is seen here at East Croydon sometime between 5 July and 18 July 1982. (A. Edwards)

A careworn No. 47511 *Thames* is seen assisting a failed and unidentified sister loco at East Croydon in July 1983. The train is 1O74, the 10.23 Manchester Piccadilly to Brighton service. By 1983 the service was formed of Mk 2 air-conditioned stock. In Platform 2 is 2EPB unit No. 5663. (A. Edwards)

A short-lived regular service was from Brighton to London Bridge via Crystal Palace and Tulse Hill. At East Croydon we find 4CIG No. 7429 forming such a service on 14 March 1981.

Running into East Croydon in August 1979 is No. 33060 with 1U21, the 17.35 London Bridge to East Grinstead service, one of a limited number of loco-hauled trains during the peaks on the Oxted line.

A southbound working in Platform 1 at East Croydon is unusual, so it's likely something is going on in this scene from 14 March 1981. 4VEG No. 7908 forms the rear of an eight-car service. An unidentified 4CIG is also southbound in the adjacent platform.

By 1984 the number of loco-hauled services on the Oxted line had dwindled to just three a day. The only evening peak service was 2L95, the 17.50 from London Bridge to East Grinstead, which we find at East Croydon powered by Class 33 No. 33007 on 5 July 1984. (G. Edwards)

Accelerating away from East Croydon is No. 47478, which appears to have sustained some minor side swipe damage when seen working 1O74, the 07.44 Manchester Piccadilly to Brighton service, in August 1979. (A. Edwards)

Approaching East Croydon station, this Class 73 has a Hastings DEMU power car in tow and is presumably en route to Selhurst Depot for repairs. (A. Edwards)

This view taken from the long demolished Essex House at Croydon in April 1979 shows an unidentified Class 73 with a long Bricklayers Arms to Brighton van train. The leading vehicle is believed to be Mk 1 Pullman Kitchen First E315 *Heron*. This coach was used to transport the Brighton and Hove Albion football team to away games when a charter train was run. (A. Edwards)

Unusual traction for a Royal Train on the Southern as an unidentified Class 31 approaches East Croydon en route from Gatwick Airport to Victoria on 22 June 1976. President Giscard d'Estaing of France was the VIP on board that day. (A. Edwards)

On 13 April 1983, 4VEG unit No. 7908 is seen stopped at South Croydon; the driver is on the phone to the signalman, presumably to find out why he has been stopped. (A. Miles)

A busy scene at South Croydon on 13 April 1983 despite the lack of passengers; are there problems ahead? From left to right we can see 4BEP unit No. 7018 in the middle of a twelve-car formation heading south and 2EPB No. 6305 leading a 4EPB unit on a service from Tattenham and Caterham to Charing Cross, while on the right 4BIG unit No. 7035 heads an eight-car formation on a Bognor to Victoria service, onto which a solitary passenger climbs. (A. Miles)

No. 73109 is captured in the cutting between East Croydon and South Croydon stations with a short train of 21-ton HTV coal hoppers on 13 April 1983. (A. Miles)

Having just arrived at Sanderstead from Elmers End in May 1983, BR 2EPB unit No. 5746 waits to shunt across to the Up line for the return journey. The line closed to passenger traffic on 13 May 1983 and the route is now largely used by Croydon Tramlink.

Also in May 1983, BR 2EPB has just shunted into the Up platform at Sanderstead to form a service to Elmers End. An Oxted eight-car loco-hauled set passes southbound en route to East Grinstead or Uckfield. The line closed to passenger traffic on 13 May 1983, though a short stub remained open for a few years to access Selsdon oil terminal.

Crossing Kenley Quarry at Riddlesdown is 3H DEMU No. 1106, which is seen leading a nine-car formation with a 3D and another 3H bringing up the rear on 15 April 1983. The train is a London Bridge to Uckfield service. (A. Miles)

Heading north near Riddlesdown on an East Grinstead to London Bridge working on 15 April 1983 we find 3H DEMU No. 1110, which has been freshly painted in blue and grey. Bringing up the rear is an all-blue 3D DEMU. (A. Miles)

With the secondman hanging out of the window, No. 33059 waits to depart Oxted station with a London Bridge to East Grinstead working in May 1983.

No. 33051 gets away from Lingfield station with an East Grinstead to London Bridge service in July 1979. Unusually, the Oxted set of eight coaches has gained an ER Mk 2 TSO as the lead vehicle. (A. Edwards)

No. 33057 double-heads a sister loco on a London Bridge to East Grinstead evening peak service in July 1979. The combination is seen approaching Lingfield station and both locomotives appear to be under power. (A. Edwards)

Arriving at Lingfield station in June 1980 with an East Grinstead to London Bridge peak service is push-pull fitted No. 33111. The eight-car Oxted sets of coaches were only used on this line from Monday to Friday. The weekends saw them stretch their legs a bit, being used on the Brighton to Cardiff and Brighton to Exeter services. (A. Edwards)

Just approaching its destination, No. 33039 arrives at East Grinstead with a peak time service from London Bridge in May 1983.

A very picturesque image of No. 33045 departing Uckfield as it crosses the River Uck with 2U27, the 19.10 to East Croydon, in May 1983. The building in the background is a former flour mill.

At Uckfield station in August 1982 we find 3D DEMU unit No. 1301 forming a service to Tonbridge and unit No. 1316, which had just arrived from London Bridge.

Crossing the A22 at Uckfield in May 1983 is No. 33054 with 2U14, the 17.20 from London Bridge. In the distance is a 3H DEMU, which is seen having just departed on the late-running 18.29 to Tonbridge.

A close study of 4SUB unit No. 4728 at Sutton station on 3 October 1973. (C. Parker)

Framed by the signal gantry at Sutton, and departing northbound from the Epsom Downs line platform, we find 4SUB No. 4387 on 3 October 1973. (C. Parker)

4SUB unit No. 4646 arrives at Epsom on a misty 16 January 1973 with a Waterloo to Horsham service. (C. Parker)

Passing northwards under the signal box at Epsom on 14 May 1977 we find Crompton No. 33035 with an excursion, allegedly from Brighton. This would have been a very unusual route, needing at least one reversal. (S. Creer)

A very forlorn-looking Coulsdon North station and 2EPB unit No. 5663 and a sister 4EPB can be seen at the nearly deserted station in October 1984.

Taken from the overgrown fast line platforms at Coulsdon North, 4CIG unit No. 7400 forms part of a Victoria to Littlehampton service via Hove in May 1984.

Clag alert! Approaching Stoats Nest Junction in August 1988, with Coulsdon South station in the background, No. 47287 has an interesting freight consisting of sand hoppers, loaded timber carriers and ferry vans. The sand hoppers probably originate from Holmethorpe Yard at Redhill and the ferry vans probably come from the Dor to Dor Depot at Crawley New Yard, but I have no idea where the timber carriers have come from.

Tucked between the Redhill and Quarry lines was Holmethorpe sand terminal. The sand quarried there was of high quality and was used for glass making. Climbing up from the yard in 1976 and heading towards Redhill we find No. 33044 with loaded HKV hoppers. 4CIG No. 7366 passes the signal box, heading to London.

Approaching Redhill station in April 1988 is a pair of Class 33s with an aggregates train. The rear loco with its distinctive crest is No. 33027 *Earl Mountbatten of Burma*.

Platform 1 at Redhill and passengers wait to join 3H unit No. 1112 while an unidentified push-pull fitted Class 33/1 sits in the siding in April 1976. (A. Edwards)

With a brand-new rake of box wagons in tow, Cromptons Nos 33023 and 33056 *The Burma Star* power through Redhill in April 1989. The line curving off to the left is to Tonbridge and to the right is the line to Reigate and Guildford.

After the 'Tadpole' DEMUs were replaced on the Tonbridge to Reading route, the Gloucester cross-country Class 119 DMUs became the stalwarts of the line. Seen in July 1982, set L593 has just arrived from Reading and will reverse at Redhill to head south to Gatwick Airport.

Powering through the centre road at Redhill in April 1989 is No. 47580 *County of Essex* with 1O66, the 07.18 Manchester Piccadilly to Brighton Inter-city service. The train sports a variety of liveries from large logo on the locomotive through to a selection of coaches in blue/grey and Intercity liveries.

A busy scene on 22 April 1979 at Earlswood, which has now been mostly buried under housing. In the yard a variety of parcels and freight stock can be seen. On the Up quarry line a CIG/BIG/CIG formation with 4CIG No. 7428 leading on a Brighton to Victoria semi-fast service can be seen, while oil tanks and an 8VEP on a Down service can be spotted in the background. (K. Oxlade)

Salfords Yard in 1979 and No. 73141 has a train of Brett Marine aggregate hoppers waiting to be unloaded.

On the Brighton main line the Peaks were very unusual visitors. On occasion one would venture south on the Brighton cross-country trains and in June 1985 eight were recorded. Awaiting the 'right away' at Gatwick on 18 June 1985, the driver of No. 45131 looks back down the train. This was 1M41, the 18.48 Brighton to Derby. The loco had worked south on 1O74, the 09.58 Manchester Piccadilly to Brighton. (A. Gibbs)

A busy scene at Gatwick Airport on 26 May 1980. With the station in the middle of a major rebuild, 4VEG unit No. 7901 waits to depart with a Bognor to Victoria service. These units were modified 4VEP units with additional luggage racks for the airport traffic.

No. 47612 *Titan* gets away from Gatwick Airport in May 1987 while working 1M50, the 09.52 Brighton to Manchester Piccadilly inter-city service. This train was routed via the West Coast Main Line and was booked to reach Manchester in just over four hours from the Sussex coast.

No. 33022 is about to pass through Gatwick Airport with a ballast train as a CIG/BIG/CIG formation departs for the coast on 22 July 1985.

A cold, bright day at Horsham on 15 February 1981 and 4EPB unit No. 5403 waits for its next working.

A wet evening at Haywards Heath and lights reflect off 2HAP No. 6044 and a sister unit, which are seen waiting to depart with the 18.28 to Seaford via Plumpton on 9 October 1981. This is a remnant of the service that used to run from Horsted Keynes to Seaford.

Seen on 13 August 1985, Seaford still sported two platforms, an electrified siding and a small traincrew depot. 4CIG unit No. 7405 waits to depart on a service back to Brighton. (R. Marsh)

Every weekend and many weekdays saw British Rail run a multitude of excursion trains across the country, offering ridiculously cheap fares for a fine day out. Accelerating away from a signal check at Keymer Junction on 31 September 1981 we find No. 47189 at Nightingale Lane, Burgess Hill. The loco is working a Hinckley to Worthing Mystex; this was a mystery day out, which often left you guessing where you would end up. (A. Gibbs)

A rather deserted Brighton station in 1986. In Platform 7 4EPB No. 5433 is waiting to be loaded with mail and parcels, while 4CIG unit No. 7381 stands in the adjacent Platform 6 and an unidentified Class 08 or 09 stands in Platform 8.

4CIG unit No. 1204, with its end door open, is seen awaiting an attachment while large logo-liveried No. 47457, with its short-lived *Ben Line* nameplate, waits to depart with the 18.05 SuO to Wolverhampton on 16 July 1989.

No. 73123 will have its work cut out later as it works 1M50, the 09.20 Brighton to Manchester Piccadilly, past Lovers Walk Depot in 1980. Hopefully the loco was replaced at Reading. (A. Gibbs)

The parcels dock at Brighton was built over when the platforms were extended and reduced in number in 1984. Back in March 1978 we find No. 09012 on the stops with No. 33050 in front, awaiting their next turn of duty. (P. Barber)

Between Lavant and Drayton, either side of Chichester, was a short-haul aggregate working. The odd French-built side discharging wagons were heavily route restricted and I believe were only cleared as far as Eastleigh for maintenance and repairs. Passing through Chichester we find No. 73120 working the empty wagons back to Lavant on 29 March 1987.

A classic 1980s line-up at Waterloo on 14 April 1984, with just the Class 33 missing for the full set. A Class 455 is seen on a suburban working, a Class 50 is on an Exeter service and 4TC No. 430 is seen leading a Bournemouth line working.

Snaking out of Waterloo, Class 50 No. 50043 *Eagle* leads 1V15, the 15.10 Waterloo to Exeter St Davids, on 11 March 1986. The station and St Paul's Cathedral dominate the skyline. (M. Hull)

2EPB units line up at Waterloo on 9 November 1981. No. 5749 is about to work a Waterloo to Waterloo service via Kingston and Richmond, while alongside is sister unit No. 5774.

An usual visitor to Clapham Junction in 1976 is this Stratford-allocated two-car Cravens Class 105 DMU. Vehicle E56143 is leading, probably on a route-learning trip.

An almost deserted platform at Clapham Junction greets 4SUB unit No. 4643 on 27 June 1980.

A complete set of Class 33 variants can be seen in this image of Clapham Junction on 30 March 1987. From left to right are a push-pull fitted Class 33/1, a standard Class 33/0, and Hastings line gauge Class 33/2 No. 33209. A variety of coaching and parcels stock fills the rest of the sidings. (M. Hull)

Passing under the impressive Clapham Junction 'A' signal box in 1980 is a pair of SR type 2EPB units, with the leading one having recently acquired blue/grey livery. The steel framework was part of air raid protection added during the Second World War and originally had cladding. (A. Gibbs)

A solitary trainspotter looks bored as No. 508002 arrives at Clapham Junction in August 1983, en route from Chessington to Waterloo. Introduced at the end of 1979, they were off the region by 1985, having been sent to Liverpool as three-car units, and were replaced on the Southern by Class 455s.

No. 455725 approaches Clapham Junction with a Waterloo to Guildford service on 1 October 1987. In Southern's waste-not tradition, this batch of Class 455s incorporated the spare trailer car from the Class 508s when they were moved to Liverpool. The ex-Class 508 coach is the second vehicle.

Crompton No. 33015 slows for Clapham Junction with 1L09, the 14.10 Waterloo to Salisbury, on 1 October 1987. The coaching stock now has a few Network SouthEast-liveried vehicles.

Just crossing over the M25 at Chertsey on 21 August 1981 is No. 47158 *Henry Ford* with a long train of 45-ton TTA oil tanks.

Rounding the curve at Woking onto the Portsmouth line on 24 September 1980 is an ICBC formation (4CIG, 4BIG, 4CIG) consisting of Nos 7408, 7057 and 7348. The train is a fast Waterloo to Portsmouth Harbour service.

4VEP No. 7823 and an unidentified 4CIG unit form a Waterloo to Portsmouth stopping service in 1980. The ensemble is seen leaving Woking. There are plenty of engineer's wagons in the yards.

Time does dull the fact that the journey from Redhill across to Reading on the Tadpole units seemed to go on forever, with all stations and only ever two – well, one and a half coaches – in use. We now look back fondly as unit No. 1206 waits to depart Guildford en route to Reading on 9 February 1979.

Tadpole DEMU Class 206 No. 1205, now sporting blue/grey livery, is snapped at Ash while working a Tonbridge to Reading service on 4 August 1980.

With Haslemere station in the background, No. 73103 hauls 4TC units Nos 428 and 427 while working the 12.16 Portsmouth Harbour to Waterloo on 9 November 1981. The same formation is noted as having worked this route a week earlier, but I have been unable to find out why it was not the usual EMU.

Passing through Bedhampton station we find No. 73105 *Quadrant* propelling LMR inspection saloon TDM395280 in July 1988. The coach is sporting the old British Railways lion and wheel coaching stock symbol.

No. 33003 trundles light engine into Fratton yard having just worked a service from Cardiff to Portsmouth Harbour on 20 June 1986. (P. Barber)

Arriving at Portsmouth Harbour with a semi fast service from Waterloo on 7 October 1981 is 4CIG No. 7352.

Across the Solent to the Isle of Wight, and from the end of steam in 1967 until they were replaced by slightly newer Underground stock from 1989, the 4VEC and 3TIS units kept the network going. With some units dating from as early as 1923, they were well past their prime before coming here. With one of the ferries from Portsmouth having just docked, in March 1975, passengers join the train at Ryde Pierhead. Solitary 4VEC unit No. 046 forms the train today.

The end of the line at Shanklin. Behind the photographer the line once continued to Ventnor. Despite the lovely summer's day, the platforms are empty as 4VEC unit No. 045 waits to depart back to Ryde Pierhead in August 1984. Maybe everyone's on the beach. (R. Marsh)

A colourful sight in Network SouthEast days as No. 50041 *Bulwark* passes through Cosham with 1O86, the 09.40 Plymouth to Portsmouth Harbour service, on 9 May 1989.

Diverted due to engineering work at Southampton, on 3 March 1984 No. 33118 is seen at Eastleigh, where it will take the normally freight-only route via Chandlers Ford to Romsey.

Stratford-allocated No. 47276 thunders through Eastleigh with 1O11, the 07.08 SO service from Bradford Exchange to Southampton, on 19 July 1980. This was one of a number of summer Friday night and Saturday services that ran from various cities such as Nottingham, Leeds and Newcastle to South Coast resorts.

An unusual image of No. 33020 and its short train of oil tanks approaching the signal at Eastleigh on 9 May 1980.

Passing through Eastleigh with a short engineer's train on 25 June 1985 is Class 73 No. 73106. Eastleigh was a great place to watch trains due to the variety of routes and services that passed through there. (P. Barber)

An ex-works No. 73112 with Mk 2 stock forms a Channel Islands boat train from Weymouth to Waterloo as it passes under the bridge at Campbell Road, Eastleigh, on 1 September 1981.

Taken from the multi-storey carpark opposite Eastleigh station on 28 April 1982, this photograph shows No. 47320 with a Freightliner service heading for the terminals at Southampton. Eastleigh Works dominates the background. The line off to the left is the route to Fareham.

Slowing for the station stop at Basingstoke, and wearing large logo livery, No. 47639 is seen working 1O15, the 09.00 Manchester Piccadilly to Poole cross-country service, on 19 April 1986. The loco had only been released from the works after its ETH conversion two months earlier. It had previously been numbered 47064. (P. Barber)

Snaking across the junction at Basingstoke is No. 33010 with an unidentified service. A 350 hp shunter and a pair of Cromptons can be seen in the stabling point. 29 September 1984.

Accelerating away from the station stop at Basingstoke is 4VEP No. 7768, seen working the 09.12 Bournemouth to Waterloo stopping service on 19 April 1986. (P. Barber)

On a bright spring day in March 1974, push-pull fitted Class 33 No. 6516 (later No. 33104) approaches Basingstoke station with an unidentified cross-country service.

Snaking across from the Reading line at Basingstoke in 1980, an unidentified Class 31 has a long parcels train in tow.

Stormy skies approach as No. 47001 slows for the station stop at Basingstoke with 1E27, the 09.55 Weymouth to Leeds cross-country service, on 3 July 1981.

With a smattering of snow on the ground, No. 47436 passes through St Denys en route to Poole with 1O15, the 08.58 from Manchester Piccadilly, on 11 February 1985. (P. Barber)

No. 33011 makes a fine sight at St Denys while working a Fawley to Eastleigh tank wagons service on 19 June 1985. (P. Barber)

No. 73101 *Brighton Evening Argus* has a light load of a couple of cement wagons and a van as it is seen approaching Mount Pleasant level crossing on the outskirts of Southampton on 1 November 1984. In the background at Bevois Park Sidings are several Rugby Cement Company lorries. (P. Barber)

Just about to pass over Mount Pleasant level crossing at Southampton is No. 31159 with an unidentified Cardiff Central to Portsmouth Harbour service on 22 September 1979.

In its heyday the Saturdays-only Brighton to the West Country service ran to twelve coaches; on this occasion in 1989, it's down to seven coaches, although the service did run on more days of the week. No. 50028 *Tiger* crosses on the Down main at Northam with 1V12, the 09.05 Brighton to Plymouth service, on 3 June 1989. (P. Barber)

At Southampton station on 16 June 1979 we find No. 47511 *Thames* with an unidentified cross-country service for Poole. The loco had only been named three months earlier on 21 March.

Diverted via Southampton due to engineering work, No. 50028 *Tiger* is on an Exeter St Davids to Waterloo service when spotted on 24 February 1985. It is formed of one of the Southern Region's eight-car Oxted sets rather than the usual Western region Mk 2 set of coaches. (P. Barber)

With exhaust smoke belching forth, No. 33037 departs Southampton with 1O65, the 06.40 Cardiff Central to Portsmouth Harbour, on 12 August 1982. Alongside is No. 33110 with a train of Bitumen tank wagons. (P. Barber)

With the large semaphore signal gantries long gone, No. 33005 departs from Southampton with an unidentified Cardiff Central to Portsmouth Harbour working on 21 February 1987. Also waiting to depart is 4REP unit No. 2001 with a Weymouth to Waterloo service.

Taken from the A33 road bridge at Millbrook, No. 47100 leads a short train of 100-ton oil tanks on 6W62, the 11.55 Furzebrook to Fawley via Southampton working, on 11 April 1988. (P. Barber)

No. 73127 glides past a great selection of 1970s and '80s cars at Redbridge while on a local trip working between Fawley and Eastleigh in August 1984.

Western Region No. 47083 *Orion* and its train of Amey Roadstone hoppers snake through Romsey Junction at Redbridge on 4 July 1984. The train is a Whatley Quarry to Totton working and the loco will run around the train at Redbridge to gain the route towards Totton. (P. Barber)

It's a beautiful day in Hampshire as No. 33043 skirts the River Test at Redbridge with 1V87, the 18.10 Portsmouth Harbour to Bristol Temple Meads, on 7 May 1987. (P. Barber)

Curving off the Bournemouth main line at Redbridge, No. 33034 and an unidentified Class 33/2 form 1V71, the 09.20 SO Brighton to Paignton, in the summer of 1982. The buffet car and locos will be detached at Exeter St Davids. The two locomotives and buffet car will then be attached to the return working. Double-heading was the norm in the summer months as the train ran to eleven or twelve carriages in length.

Salisbury was the limit of one of the very cheap Southern Region Runabout tickets; the eastern limit was, weirdly, East Worthing. I usually got one during the school holidays. Here in the summer of 1975 we find No. 31250 on a Portsmouth Harbour to Cardiff Central working, making a connection with No. 33105 on a Waterloo to Exeter St Davids service. This joined-up thinking happened every two hours through the day. (A. Gibbs)

Leap forward eight years and the cascade of motive power is clear to see. No. 50036 *Victorious* along with the rest of the class is working the Waterloo to Exeter route while the Cromptons have been relegated to the Portsmouth to Cardiff route. No. 33008 *Eastleigh* makes the connection today, 22 June 1983. (P. Barber)

A pair of Class 31s approaches Salisbury with a Cardiff Central to Portsmouth Harbour working in the summer of 1978.

Headcode 11 signifies the Brighton to Exeter St Davids service. At Salisbury we see No. 33047 waiting to depart with 1V71, the 09.20 SO from Brighton, on 9 April 1983. The eight-coach train in the winter months was light enough for a single locomotive.

Push-pull fitted No. 33101 rolls into Salisbury with a Waterloo to Exeter St Davids service on 29 September 1987. The poor performance of the Class 50s meant that the Cromptons regularly covered services on this route.

Wilton Junction near Salisbury was the boundary of the Southern and Western Regions. With a Portsmouth Harbour to Cardiff Central service, No. 33058 takes the route towards Westbury in 1983. The Exeter line is to the right.

There is plenty of snow on the ground at Foxhills crossing near Ashurst in the New Forest as No. 73104, with one of the temporary 4TCB units and a 4TC unit, makes good time on this Weymouth to Waterloo service on 19 March 1987.

4TC No. 8001 leads a 4REP unit through the New Forest at Beaulieu Road on a Waterloo to Weymouth service in August 1986. (M. Hull)

Working a stopping service from Bournemouth to Waterloo in August 1986 is 4VEP No. 7735. The service is captured near Beaulieu Road in the New Forest. (M. Hull)

No. 47406 *Railriders* was named after the children's club that British Rail launched in 1981. Here we find the locomotive about to depart Bournemouth with 1M20, the 14.58 Poole to Liverpool Lime Street, on 15 May 1987. (I. J. Stewart)

Look out, there's a train behind you! Two members of staff walk the Weymouth tramway to check for obstructions – mainly parked cars and vans – as No. 33114 slowly follows them with the boat train from Waterloo to connect with the Sealink ferry to the Channel Islands in November 1986.